Stories
of
GREAT PEOPLE

# Mother Teresa's alms bowl

Anita Ganeri

llustrated by Leighton Noyes
and Karen Radford

🌱 Crabtree Publishing Company
www.crabtreebooks.com

Mr. RUMMAGE has a stall piled high with interesting objects—and he has a great story to tell about each and every one of his treasures.

DIGBY PLATT is an antique collector. Every Saturday he picks up a bargain at Mr. Rummage's antique stall and loves listening to the story behind his new 'find'.

HANNAH PLATT is Digby's argumentative, older sister— and she doesn't believe a word that Mr. Rummage says!

SAFFRON sells pots and pans, herbs, spices, oils, soaps, and dyes from her spice kitchen stall.

# Crabtree Publishing Company
www.crabtreebooks.com

## Other books in the series

Shakespeare's quill

Cleopatra's Coin

Columbus's chart

Martin Luther King, Jr.'s microphone

Leonardo's palette

Armstrong's moon rock

The Wright Brothers' glider

Marco Polo's silk purse

Sitting Bull's tomahawk

**Library and Archives Canada Cataloguing in Publication**

Ganeri, Anita, 1961-
        Mother Teresa's alms bowl / Anita Ganeri ; illustrated by
Leighton Noyes and Karen Radford.

(Stories of great people)
Includes index.
ISBN 978-0-7787-3689-9 (bound).--ISBN 978-0-7787-3712-4 (pbk.)

        1. Teresa, Mother, 1910-1997--Juvenile fiction. 2. Missionaries of
Charity--Biography--Juvenile fiction. 3. Nuns--India--Calcutta--
Biography--Juvenile fiction. I. Noyes, Leighton II. Radford, Karen
III. Title. IV. Series.

PZ7.G15Mo 2008              j813'.6              C2007-907626-2

**Library of Congress Cataloging-in-Publication Data**

Ganeri, Anita, 1961-
   Mother Teresa's alms bowl / Anita Ganeri ; illustrated by Leighton Noyes and
Karen Radford.
      p. cm. -- (Stories of great people)
   Includes index.
   ISBN-13: 978-0-7787-3690-5 (rlb)
   ISBN-10: 0-7787-3690-3 (rlb)
   ISBN-13: 978-0-7787-3712-4 (pb)
   ISBN-10: 0-7787-3712-8 (pb)
   1. Teresa, Mother, 1910-1997--Juvenile literature. 2. Missionaries of Charity--
Biography--Juvenile literature. 3. Nuns--India--Calcutta--Biography--Juvenile
literature. I. Noyes, Leighton. II. Radford, Karen. III. Title. IV. Series.

BX4406.5.Z8G26 2008
271'.97--dc22
[B]
                                                    2007050988

# Crabtree Publishing Company
www.crabtreebooks.com          1-800-387-7650

**Published in Canada**
**Crabtree Publishing**
616 Welland Ave.
St. Catharines, Ontario
L2M 5V6

**Published in the United States**
**Crabtree Publishing**
PMB16A
350 Fifth Ave., Suite 3308
New York, NY  10118

**Published by CRABTREE PUBLISHING COMPANY**
Copyright © 2008 Diverta Ltd.

# Mother Teresa's Alms Bowl

## Table of Contents

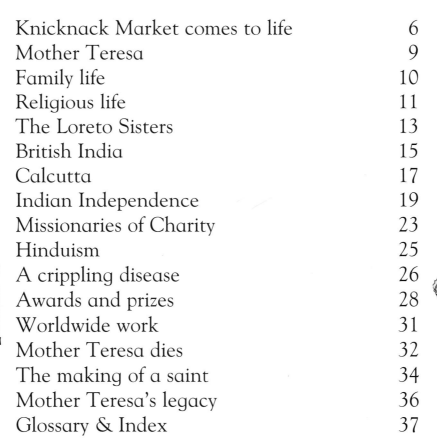

Every Saturday morning, Knicknack Market comes to life. The street vendors are there almost before the sun is up. And by the time you and I are out of bed, the stalls are built, the boxes are opened, and all the goods are carefully laid out on display.

Objects are piled high. Some are laid out on velvet: precious knecklaces and jeweled swords. Others stand upright at the back: large, framed pictures of very important people, lamps made from tasseled satin, and old-fasioned cash registers—the kind that jingle when the drawers are opened.

And then there are the things that stay in their boxes all day, waiting for the right customer to come along: war medals laid out in straight lines, stopwatches on leather straps, and utensils in polished silver for all those special occasions.

But Mr. Rummage's stall is different. Mr. Rummage of Knicknack Market has a stall piled high with a disorderly jumble of things that no one could ever want. Who'd want to buy a stuffed mouse? Or a broken umbrella? Or a pair of false teeth?

Well, Mr. Rummage has them all. And, as you can imagine, they don't cost much!

**D**igby Platt, ten-year-old collector of antiques, was on his way to see his friend Mr. Rummage of Knicknack Market. It was Saturday, and as usual, Digby's weekly allowance was burning a hole in his pocket.

But Digby wasn't going to spend his money on any old thing. It had to be something rare and interesting for his collection, something from Mr. Rummage's incredible stall.

Hannah, Digby's older sister, had come to the market too. She always kept an eye on Digby's visits there.

She had secret doubts about the value of Mr. Rummage's objects, and felt, for some big-sisterly reason, that she had to stop her little brother from buying useless junk.

As Hannah and Digby approached Mr. Rummage's stall, they found him hard at work with a cloth, polishing a small, battered, brass bowl.

"Hi there, kids," said Mr. Rummage, blowing on the bowl and rubbing hard. "I'll be with you in a moment. I just want to get this bowl nice and shiny for my collection."

"What are you collecting, Mr. Rummage?" asked Hannah, suspiciously. Glancing around Mr. Rummage's stall, she didn't think he needed any more old junk.

"I'm collecting for charity," replied Mr. Rummage, giving the gleaming bowl one last rub. "I'm going to put this bowl on the counter and then people can put their spare change in it."

"It looks pretty battered," said Digby, peering closely at the bowl. "Wouldn't a nice, new bowl be better?"

"Oh, but this is no ordinary bowl," said a soft voice from behind him. "It's an Indian **alms** bowl."

"Hi Saffron," said Hannah. "What's an alms bowl?"

"It's a bowl that holy people in India use to collect donations of money, food, and other things," replied Saffron, smiling.

"Yes, and this particular alms bowl," continued Mr. Rummage, "belonged to a very holy person. Her name was Mother Teresa. She became a nun and spent her life helping the poorest people in India and around the world. One of her jobs was to go from house to house collecting leftover food for the poor to eat."

Mother Teresa was born Agnes Bojaxhiu on August 26, 1910 in Skopje, a town that today lies in the country known as Macedonia. Her parents, Nikola and Drana, had three children—Lazar (a boy), Age (a girl), and Agnes. Agnes was the youngest. Her family called her Gonxha, which means "flower bud." When she became a **nun** she changed her name to Teresa.

In the 20th century, Mother Teresa became one of the most famous and admired women in the world. In 1948, she founded a religious order of nuns, called the Missionaries of Charity, in Calcutta, India. Through this order, she dedicated her life to the poor, sick, and dying, in India and around the world.

## Let's find out more...

An alms bowl is used to collect money and food to give to poor people.

# Family life

Agnes's father was a merchant and her family was fairly well off. Her father

Agnes as a young girl

owned several houses, and the family lived in one of them. Agnes went to the local primary school, then to secondary school.

She did well at her studies and was particularly good at writing and music. But Agnes's happy family life was suddenly shattered in 1919, when her father died.

Agnes's mother couldn't manage the family's business and the family lost everything, except their home. Agnes' mother, a devout Christian, told her children that possessions and belongings weren't important. It was much more important to live an unselfish life.

There are many different pictures of Mary, the mother of Jesus.

## The Roman Catholic Church

The Roman Catholic Church is one of the main branches of Christianity. About half of all Christians today are Roman Catholics. The head of the Roman Catholic Church is the pope whose headquarters are in the Vatican City in Rome. The word pope means "father." Roman Catholics believe that the pope takes the place of Jesus's disciple, Peter, who led the first Christians and was the first bishop of Rome. Roman Catholics pray to God, to Jesus, and also to the Blessed Virgin Mary, Jesus's mother. Many Roman Catholic churches have statues or pictures of Mary and other **saints**—people who have lived especially holy lives.

## Religious life

Agnes's family members were devout Roman Catholics. Her mother tried to put her Christian faith into practice by opening her house to the poor and needy. She and her three children prayed together every evening and attended the local church, called the Sacred Heart of Jesus. Agnes and her sister sang in the church choir and took part in many church activities.

During her early years, Agnes was fascinated by stories of the lives of missionaries, or people who travelled and helped spread the Roman Catholic religion. By the time she was twelve, she was convinced that she too wanted to commit herself to a religious life.

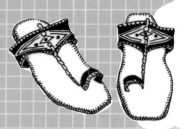

Indian sandals

Montenegro is a country of mountains and lakes.

## To the mountains

Once a year, the family made a **pilgrimage** to the shrine of the Madonna of Letnice in the mountains of Montenegro where they prayed in the little chapel. This was also the family's annual vacation. It was hoped that the mountain air would help Agnes's poor health.

Agnes with her brother and sister

"Whatever!" muttered Digby. "What happened next, Mr. Rummage?"

"Well, on October 13, 1928, Agnes and another girl set off from the city of Zagreb on the long train ride across Europe to Paris. Agnes's mother and sister came to send them off."

"Did she pass the interview?" asked Hannah.

"Yes," said Mr. Rummage. "Both girls were accepted as novices, or new nuns. From Paris, they were sent to Loreto Abbey near Dublin in Ireland. Agnes never saw her mother again."

"They must have felt very homesick," said Hannah. "I mean, they were a long way from home."

"Yes," agreed Mr. Rummage, "but they were kept very busy at the abbey. They had just six weeks to learn English, a language they'd never spoken before. Luckily, Agnes was good at languages and soon picked it up."

"**H**ow did Agnes become a nun?" asked Hannah. "Are there special nun schools?"

"Not exactly," chuckled Mr. Rummage. "Agnes applied to join a group of nuns called the Loreto Sisters. She chose them because she knew they worked in India. Agnes was very excited when the Mother Superior invited her for an interview in Paris."

"I don't know what a Mother Superior is," said Digby. "But it sure sounds scary!"

"A Mother Superior is a head nun," said Hannah, looking pleased with herself. "I saw one in a movie."

# The Loreto Sisters

The Order of the Sisters of Loreto, or the Loreto Sisters, is the common name for the Institute of the Blessed Virgin Mary. The order was founded in 1609 by Mary Ward, an English Roman Catholic nun. Mary joined a convent of the Poor Clares in France, but decided that God was calling her to lead a more active life. She began to recruit other nuns to set up and run schools for girls.

Mary was strongly criticized by the Catholic Church because her nuns did not wear habits or live in a convent. But her work continued and, in 1822, the Institute was given a house outside Dublin which was named Loreto Abbey. The order flourished in Ireland and, in 1841, the Loreto Sisters were asked to begin teaching and nursing in India.

Mary Ward (1585-1645), was an English Roman Catholic nun who founded the Loreto Sisters.

## Religious orders

The Loreto Sisters are one of several religious orders of nuns in the Roman Catholic Church. Catholic nuns believe that they are "brides of Christ" and take vows of poverty, chastity, and obedience. They live as part of an order, or religious community. Some nuns live mainly in a convent and have little contact with the outside world. Others may work as nurses or teachers. Whichever order they belong to, nuns lead strict lives of prayer and self-sacrifice, devoted to God. There are also similar orders for priests and monks.

Loreto Abbey near Dublin

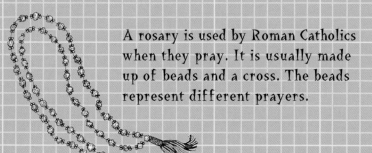

A rosary is used by Roman Catholics when they pray. It is usually made up of beads and a cross. The beads represent different prayers.

13

"**W**hen did Agnes get to go to India?" asked Hannah, impatiently.

"On the first of December," said Mr. Rummage, "the two girls left Ireland and began their long journey to India. At that time, there weren't any airplanes so they had to go by boat."

"How long did it take?" asked Digby.

"It took about four weeks," replied Mr. Rummage. "And Agnes wasn't called Agnes anymore. She'd chosen the name Sister Teresa, after a saint called Teresa of Lisieux. She was a French nun who believed the best way to do God's work was by doing small, simple tasks and doing them cheerfully."

"Agnes, I mean, Sister Teresa must have been glad to get there," said Hannah.

"She was," agreed Mr. Rummage. "But it was very different to what she was used to at home. Her first stop was Colombo in Sri Lanka. She wrote many letters to her family, describing the heat, the crowded streets, and the tropical palm trees."

"Look, I found Colombo!" said Digby, excitedly, pointing to an old globe he'd found among Mr. Rummage's junk.

"Excellent, Digby, now can you find Chennai in India?" said Mr. Rummage. "It was called Madras when Sister Teresa arrived there. She was shocked to see how terribly poor the people were. She knew that if people back home could see this poverty, they would stop grumbling about their own problems. Anyway, after a stop in Calcutta, the nuns reached Darjeeling."

"What did they do there?" asked Hannah. "They spent the next two years learning to live according to the rules of the Loreto Sisters," said Mr. Rummage. "Just before her twenty-first birthday, Sister Teresa took her vows, or promises, of chastity, poverty, and obedience. From then on, there was no going back to her former life."

# British India

In 1928, when Agnes first arrived in India, the country was still ruled by Britain. The British had set up the East India Company in 1600 to trade Indian goods, such as tea, spices, cotton, and indigo. Gradually, the power of the company grew and it turned from trading in Indian goods to taking over huge areas of Indian land. Soon, large parts of India came under British rule. In 1858, the Company was abolished and the British government took direct control of India. This was the beginning of British rule, or Raj, as it was known. It continued until August 1947, when India became an independent country.

## Life in Darjeeling

Darjeeling was a town in northeast India found in the foothills of the Himalayan mountains. Nicknamed the "Queen of the Hills," it was the town in which many British people spent the hot summer months. Surrounded by tea plantations, it had large houses and nice hotels, cooling breezes, and stunning views. It was also used as a hospital for British troops. It was in this beautiful setting that Sister Teresa completed her training. She studied religion, read the Bible, and learned the Indian languages of Hindi and Bengali. She also taught in the convent school and helped in a small hospital where she nursed some of the poorest people. Sister Teresa was remembered as being hard-working and jolly.

An old print of Darjeeling in the 1920s shows workers on a tea plantation.

an old Indian teapot

"So where did Sister Teresa go next?" asked Digby.

"She went back to Calcutta," replied Saffron, taking up the story. "It's one of the biggest cities in India."

"Got it!" yelled Digby, jabbing his finger on his globe.

"Sister Teresa was sent to work at the Loreto School in the Entally district of east Calcutta. She taught geography and history to girls."

"Was she a good teacher?" asked Hannah.

"She was," said Saffron. "She enjoyed her work and her pupils liked her very much. All the lessons were in English but later she moved to another school, called St. Mary's. This school taught girls from poorer families and the lessons were in Bengali. She must have been happy because she stayed there for 17 years!

Then, in 1935, Sister Teresa went to teach at a primary school in a desperately poor area. She was shocked to see the awful conditions there. But things were even worse in other places.

Every Sunday, she visited poor people in the Motijhil **slum**."

"What's a slum?" asked Hannah.

"It's a very poor and overcrowded part of a city where people live in makeshift houses made of tin, mud, or even cardboard. Often there's no running water or electricity and no toilets. Life in a slum is very hard.

Then, on May 14, 1937, she took her final vows and became Mother Teresa. And that's how most people know her."

# Calcutta

The city of Calcutta began as a small village built on swampy marshland along the banks of the Hooghly River. In 1686, British merchants set up a trading post at the village. At first, the post wasn't a success but in 1696, a fort was built and after that, Calcutta grew steadily into a major port.

In 1756, Calcutta was captured by the local ruler, but the British won it back the following year. A much larger fort was built and Calcutta became the capital of British India until 1911. Today, Calcutta is the capital of the state of Bengal and is called Kolkata, its old Bengali name.

In the 1800s and early 1900s, Calcutta had grand buildings.

## Poverty and palaces

As the capital of British India, Calcutta grew wealthy. It had impressive government buildings, together with clubs, hotels, and stores for British officials and their families. But not far from these buildings were **squalid** back streets where the poorest people of the city lived. Even the convent Mother Teresa stayed in was in a large, peaceful compound, very different from the stinking slums sprawling just outside its walls.

In the early days of British rule, grand processions were held on the streets of Calcutta.

Today, there are still many slum areas in Calcutta.

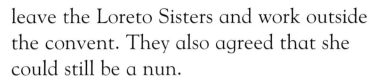

"Mother Teresa didn't stay a teacher forever," Mr. Rummage went on. "Things changed when she fell ill in September of 1946.
She was sent to Darjeeling to get better, but on the train trip, an amazing thing happened."

"What was that, Mr. Rummage?" asked Digby and Hannah at the same time.

"Mother Teresa called it 'a call within a call,'" replied Mr. Rummage. "She was sure she heard God's voice telling her to leave the convent and live among the poorest of the poor.

But she needed permission to leave the Loreto Sisters. The Archbishop of Calcutta didn't like the idea of her wandering the dangerous streets of Calcutta on her own. He tried to make her change her mind."

"And did she?" asked Hannah.

Mr. Rummage shook his head. "She was more determined than ever! At last the Church authorities in Delhi agreed to let her leave the Loreto Sisters and work outside the convent. They also agreed that she could still be a nun.

It was difficult to leave the safety of the order after so many years. Besides, she had to give up her Loreto habit and find something else to wear! She decided to dress like a Bengali woman. So she went to the market and bought a plain white cotton **sari** with a blue border, and some simple sandals. She pinned a **crucifix** to her left shoulder."

# Indian independence

Independence Day celebrations in India, 1947

## Hindu-Muslim violence

In the 1930s and 40s, there was a lot of turmoil in India. Many Indians were working hard to win freedom for their country. They wanted the British to leave the government in their hands. But this caused trouble between India's two main religions—Hinduism and Islam. **Muslims** were afraid that Hindus would take control of an independent India. They demanded that part of India should become their own country—Pakistan. On August 16, 1946, Muslims protested on the streets of Calcutta. The result was a bloodbath. Thousands of Hindus and Muslims were killed in the violence.

## Partition of India

The British government decided that the only way to stop the violence was to give India independence. They would also divide the country into Hindu and Muslim parts. At midnight on August 14-15, 1947, India became free. But it was impossible to divide it neatly into Hindu India and Muslim Pakistan. So the states of Punjab in the west and Bengal in the east were split along religious lines. This left the two mainly Muslim areas—renamed West and East Pakistan—on opposite sides of the country. Many people found themselves on the wrong side of the borders and fled for their lives. In the chaos that followed, millions were killed in Hindu-Muslim violence. Millions more became refugees, many of whom poured into already overcrowded Calcutta.

India was divided into three parts: India, West Pakistan and East Pakistan.

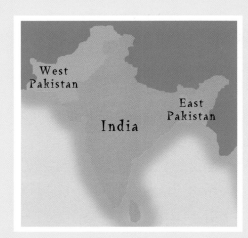

# A place to stay

As Mother Teresa's school became more popular, she needed a bigger building to live and work in. Luckily an Indian Roman Catholic, called Michael Gomes, offered her a large room in his home at 14 Creek Lane—and it was rent-free.

Indian chair

Poor families flocked to Creek Lane to ask for Mother Teresa's help.

## Bless this house!

Mother Teresa moved into her new home in February of 1949. She brought with her a bench, a box for a table, a chair, and a cupboard, which she used as an altar. She was also given a bed.

Now, at last, she had a base for her work and space for others to come and join her.

Michael Gomes later gave her two larger rooms to use. He was happy to help. He believed that having Mother Teresa in his home was a great blessing.

Indian cabinet

Indian goblet

## Food for the poor

When people heard what Mother Teresa was doing, they gave her money and came to help. She also went from door to door, with her alms bowl, asking people for any leftover food to give to the poor and hungry. But Mother Teresa never worried too much about not having enough money or food. She always believed that God would provide her with everything she needed.

"In December of 1948, Mother Teresa returned to Calcutta and just before Christmas, she finally began working in the slums," Mr. Rummage continued. "She decided to start her work in the Motijhil slum, which she knew because it was next to her old school of St. Mary's."

"What did she do there?" asked Digby.

"She opened a school for the children," said Mr. Rummage. "Many of them had never been to school before. Often they had to work instead in order to help their families."

"That's terrible," said Hannah, quietly. "What was the school like?"

"Well, it didn't have any classrooms, or even chairs or desks," Mr. Rummage replied. "In fact, it was just an open space between houses. The children squatted on the ground and Mother Teresa scratched the letters of the alphabet in the dust with a stick."

"Did the children like going to school?" asked Digby doubtfully.

"They loved it," smiled Mr. Rummage.

"There were 21 pupils on the first day, and twice that many the next day. Numbers went up steadily and by January, Mother Teresa had more than 50 pupils and three teachers helping her. Soon she was able to rent a small shelter, which became a classroom."

"What other work did Mother Teresa do?" asked Hannah.

"Well, she began visiting the many poor and sick people who lived in the slums," said Mr. Rummage. "It was hard, and sometimes upsetting, work. Once, Mother Teresa met a man with a badly injured thumb. The thumb needed removing, so she took a pair of scissors and cut it off. It's said that the man fainted one way, and Mother Teresa fainted the other! Oh dear, are you feeling okay, Hannah? You're looking a little pale."

"Do you think Mother Teresa ever got lonely?" asked Hannah.

"She might have been but she wasn't on her own for long," said Saffron, taking up the story. (A customer had come to Mr. Rummage's stall and he didn't get many of those!) "Soon, a girl called Subhasini Das came to join her. She'd been one of Mother Teresa's pupils at St. Mary's and, like her teacher, wanted to help the poor. She later took the name of Sister Agnes. Then, two months later, two more girls followed. They took the names of Sister Gertrude and Sister Margaret Mary. They helped Mother Teresa teach the children in the school, and look after the sick and dying people in the slums."

"Did they become nuns, too?" asked Digby.

"Yes," replied Saffron. "In October of 1950, Mother Teresa set up her own order of nuns called the Missionaries of Charity. She became head of the Order, and the girls who joined her were known as "Sisters.""

"Creek Lane must have been getting quite crowded!" said Hannah.

"It was," smiled Saffron. "Especially as more Sisters joined the Order over the next two years. Soon the house was too crowded. It was clear they needed somewhere bigger to live, but it was difficult finding somewhere cheap enough for them to rent. Of course, Mother Teresa wasn't worried. She was sure that God would help them."

"And did he?" asked Digby, eagerly. "Help them, I mean?"

"It certainly looked that way," replied Saffron. "By chance, Mother Teresa found out about a house on Lower Circular Road, one of the main roads in Calcutta. It was owned by a Muslim man but because of the trouble between Muslims and Hindus, he'd decided to move to Pakistan. He agreed to sell it to the Missionaries of Charity for a cheap price and in February of 1953, they moved in. The house became the headquarters of the Missionaries of Charity and was known as the Mother House. And, amazingly, it's still the Mother House of the Order today."

# Missionaries of Charity

## Joining the Order

When a girl joined the Missionaries of Charity, she was expected to devote her life to helping the poor. The nuns wore the same habit as Mother Teresa—a white sari with blue borders and a small crucifix. Apart from this, they had very few belongings—two cotton saris, a pair of sandals, a crucifix, a prayer book, an umbrella, a thin mattress, and a metal bucket for washing themselves and their clothes.

## A day in the life

The sisters' days followed a strict routine. They got up at 4:40 a.m, got washed and dressed, and cleaned their teeth with ash from the kitchen stove. From 5:15 to 6:45, there was morning prayer. For breakfast, they had cold milk and five chapatis (flat Indian bread), and by 7:45 am, they were out at work. At noon, they returned to the Mother House for prayers and lunch. Afterward, they did housework and had a short rest. Then it was back to their duties in the city. At six, they went home for a dinner of rice, lentils, and vegetables. Then there was time for light chores and relaxation, until bed at 10 p.m.

"Mother Teresa worked very hard," said Digby.

"Probably," said Mr. Rummage. "But there was too much work to do to rest. She opened a home where poor and sick people could die in peace. In Calcutta, thousands of people were homeless and lived on the city streets. And that's also where they died, often with no one to look after them."

"How awful," said Hannah, sadly. "Why couldn't they go to a hospital?"

"Most of the hospitals were full, and besides, these people were too poor to pay for medicine," said Mr. Rummage. "Mother Teresa wanted somewhere they could die in peace. Luckily, the city authorities wanted to help," Mr. Rummage went on. "So they offered her a house next to a temple dedicated to the Hindu goddess, Kali. The house was dirty and run down, but Mother Teresa accepted immediately. She called the home Nirmal Hriday, which means the place of the 'pure heart.'"

"It must have been hard to see people dying and in pain," said Hannah.

"It was," agreed Mr. Rummage. "But Mother Teresa believed that everyone had the right to 'die beautifully,' or to spend their last days feeling loved and looked after."

"Even then Mother Teresa didn't rest," smiled Saffron, taking up the story. "She found another old house, close to the Mother House, and she turned it into a home for unwanted children. She called it Shishu Bhavan, which means "the children's home." It was opened in September of 1955 and had space for 90 children."

"Why didn't anyone want the children?" asked Digby.

"Well, sometimes their parents were too poor to look after them," said Saffron. "They just couldn't afford food or clothes. And sometimes their parents had died and they were left as orphans."

# Hinduism

Most people in India are Hindus. They follow the ancient religion of Hinduism, which began at least 4,000 years ago. Most Hindus believe in a great spirit, called Brahman or God. They also believe in hundreds of gods and goddesses who represent Brahman's many powers. The Kali Temple, where Mother Teresa's home, Nirmal Hriday, was set up, was one of the holiest places in Calcutta for Hindus.

## Kali the goddess

The fierce-looking Kali is the Hindu goddess of death. She stands for the frightening side of life which people must face and overcome. Kali is shown wearing a tiger skin, with fang-like teeth and a necklace of human skulls. Her skin is usually black. The Kalighat temple in Calcutta is her main temple. Here, sheep and goats are regularly sacrificed to the goddess. It is such a sacred place that devout Hindus hope to be cremated, or burned to ashes, there when they die.

Kali, the Hindu goddess of death.

An old house in the city of Calcutta was turned into a school.

## Helping each other

Some Hindus weren't happy to have Christian nuns working next to their temple. They were afraid that they would try to convert dying people to Christianity. The Hindu priests organized protests against the sisters. But when the Sisters took in a dying Hindu priest, they were finally accepted by their neighbors.

Mother Teresa helped many children from the slums.

# A crippling disease

Leprosy is an infectious disease caused by a bacteria. It deforms parts of the body, and damages the skin and nerves. One of the first signs of the disease are light spots on the skin, which may develop into lumps. If the disease is not treated, it can cause paralysis and loss of fingers and toes.

Because these symptoms are so unpleasant, lepers were thought to be unclean and were made to live apart from other people. Millions of people still suffer from leprosy, particularly in poorer countries, such as India. But the disease can be treated with drugs if it is caught early, and many people have been cured.

Mother Teresa visited hospitals and gave comfort to the sick and dying.

"But there was another group of people whom Mother Teresa wanted to help," continued Saffron. "And they needed her help very badly."

"Who were they?" asked Hannah.

"They were **lepers**," replied Saffron. "People who suffer from a dreadful disease called **leprosy**. At that time, many people were frightened of lepers spreading the disease. So lepers often had to leave their homes and live apart from other people. They had no jobs, so they were forced to beg on the streets. Many were so ashamed of their illness, they tried to hide away."

"Poor people," said Digby softly. "Was Mother Teresa able to help them?"

"She was, Digby," said Saffron. "She opened a shelter for lepers at Gobra on the edge of the city. But it only had space for about 150 of the 30,000 lepers in Calcutta. A few months later, she set up a clinic at Shishu Bhavan where lepers could come to get medicine to treat their disease.

Soon afterward, the shelter at Gobra was closed down because the land was needed for building. Mother Teresa tried desperately to find another place but it wasn't easy. Nobody wanted lepers living close by."

"What did she do?" asked Hannah. "She couldn't let all those people down."

"She set up a mobile leprosy clinic instead!" said Saffron. "With money that was donated, she bought two vans and filled them with medicines and food. The vans drove around the slums, handing out the medicine."

"What a great idea!" said Digby. "That way plenty of people were helped."

"But Mother Teresa still wanted a permanent place where lepers could live and work," Saffron went on. "The Missionaries of Charity were already working at a leper community at Titagarh on the outskirts of Calcutta and Mother Teresa was given some land to build a new clinic there. Even so, another community was badly needed.

Then Mother Teresa had a stroke of luck. The Indian government gave her a large plot of land about 200 miles (320 km) from Calcutta. She raffled off a car given to her by the pope to raise funds, and began to build a leper community. She called it Shanti Nagar, which means "the place of peace." Here, hundreds of lepers were able to live normal lives. They helped to build their own houses, grew their own rice, and ran their own grocery store. They also made baskets for sale and even started a printing press. This meant they did not have to beg and could look after themselves."

# Awards and prizes

## Lotuses and jewels

Throughout the 1960s and 1970s, Mother Teresa received many awards and prizes from governments and organizations around the world, and from the pope in Rome. Among the most precious were those awarded by the Indian government for her work among the Indian people.

In 1962, Mother Teresa was awarded the Padma Shree (Respected Lotus), one of the highest honors given to Indian citizens. The lotus is the national flower of India and it is sacred An even greater honor, came in 1980. Mother Teresa was awarded the Bharat Ratna (Jewel of India), India's highest award. This award recognizes "public service of the highest order."

Mother Teresa met Pope John Paul II in Rome, Italy.

## Nobel Peace Prize

Mother Teresa and the Nobel Peace Prize

The Nobel Peace Prize is awarded every year to a person who has worked hard to make the world a peaceful place. In 1979, Mother Teresa won the prize. The cash award was set aside to build more houses for lepers.

 ## Special celebrations

In December, she flew to Oslo in Norway for the glittering prize-giving ceremony. Wearing her simple cotton sari and sandals, as usual, Mother Teresa said that she herself was unworthy of the prize but accepted it on behalf of "the poorest of the poor of the world." Afterwards, she asked for a banquet in her honor to be canceled and the money given to the poor. The celebrations didn't end there. When she arrived back in India, a reception was held for her in the Red Fort in Delhi. Only two other Indians had been given this honor before her—Jawaharlal Nehru and Indira Gandhi, both prime ministers of India.

"Did Mother Teresa ever get a vacation?" asked Digby.

"Not exactly a vacation," smiled Mr. Rummage, taking up the story. "But in 1960, she went to the United States. It was her first trip since she arrived in India. After that, she visited Britain, Germany, Switzerland, and Italy, promoting her work and raising funds."

"She was quite a globetrotter!" said Hannah.

"Yes, Hannah," said Mr. Rummage, "and the trip was just the beginning.

She spent the rest of her life traveling to different countries, making speeches, accepting awards, and opening new houses."

"She must have become very famous," said Digby.

"She was," agreed Mr. Rummage. "And in 1969, she became even more famous. A British journalist, called Malcolm Muggeridge, came to Calcutta to make a movie about her work. It was called *Something Beautiful for God*. When the movie was shown, Mother Teresa became a superstar!"

"Did being famous make her different?" asked Hannah. "Sometimes it goes to people's heads."

"No," said Mr. Rummage. "She was always very humble. When someone asked her about the amazing work she'd done, she replied it was God's work, not hers."

"I wish I'd been able to meet Mother Teresa," sighed Digby. "I wonder what she was really like."

"I wish I'd met her, too," said Mr. Rummage. "She's always been a great heroine of mine. She was tiny—about five feet (1.5 m) tall—but she was incredibly energetic and strong minded. Some of the places she visited were dangerous, so she also had to be very brave. Once she visited the Middle East during a war between the Israelis and Palestinians. There, she persuaded the two sides to stop fighting just long enough for her to rescue 37 patients from a hospital!"

"I could never have done that," said Hannah, admiringly.

"That's for sure," laughed Digby. "You're even scared of spiders!"

"When people asked Mother Teresa where she got her courage from, she said she got it from God," said Mr. Rummage. "She believed that God guided her in all she did. She once said, 'I am like a little pencil in God's hand. He does the thinking. He does the writing. The pencil has only to be allowed to be used.'"

"Did everyone like her?"

asked Hannah. "Or did some people think she was a goody-goody?"

"Good question, Hannah," said Mr. Rummage. "Some people didn't like Mother Teresa. They said that, for all her good work, she didn't do anything to try to get rid of poverty once and for all. They also criticized the poor medical care in her houses and the fact that she was so busy traveling she didn't have time to get involved with poor people anymore."

"What did Mother Teresa say about that?" asked Digby.

"She genuinely felt she was doing God's work," said Mr. Rummage. "So she took no notice of the criticism. She used to say, 'No matter who says what, you should accept it with a smile and do your own work.'"

# Worldwide work

## Missionaries abroad

At first, the Missionaries of Charity were only allowed to work in Calcutta. Later, they opened houses in other Indian cities, such as Delhi and Mumbai (Bombay), where there were also slums. In 1965, the pope allowed Mother Teresa to open houses in other countries. The first was opened in Venezuela and many more soon followed in Africa, Australia, Asia, North America, and Europe. In 1980, a house was opened in Skopje, Mother Teresa's hometown. It was difficult for the Sisters living so far from home. Many felt homesick and struggled to get used to a different language and culture. Even so, Mother Teresa expected them to do their work cheerfully and willingly.

The Missionaries of Charity has spread all over the world.

## Missionary Brothers

In 1963, a new branch of the Missionaries of Charity was founded. It was called the Missionary Brothers of Charity. The two orders worked closely together. The first Brothers were priests who lived in Shishu Bhavan, the children's home in Calcutta. They looked after homeless boys living in the city's train stations. Later, they ran the Titagarh leper community. The head of the brothers was an Australian priest, called Father Andrew. His helpers wore ordinary shirts and pants, instead of religious clothing. A small crucifix pinned to their shirts was all that showed they were brothers.

# Mother Teresa dies

Despite years of hard work, Mother Teresa seemed unstoppable. Although she was frail and bent, and often ill, she always returned to her work. When she was asked why she did not rest more, she replied, "There will be plenty of time to rest in eternity. Here there is so much to do…" But in 1983, she suffered heart problems during a visit to Pope John Paul II in Rome and was forced to rest. After this, her health became more fragile.

Mother Teresa's funeral ceremony

## Sister Nirmala

By 1996, Mother Teresa was seriously ill and elections were held to find out who would take over as head of the order. Sister Nirmala was chosen as the new leader. She was 63 years old, kind, and wise. She came from a Hindu family in Nepal. Mother Teresa was very pleased with the choice.

Mother Teresa's grave

## State funeral

Despite her frailness, Mother Teresa visited Rome and the United States again in May of 1997. It was to be her last tour. On September 5, 1997, a few days after her eightyseventh birthday, Mother Teresa died of a heart attack. Hearing the news, the French president said, "This evening, there is less love, less compassion, less light in the world." A week later, she was given a state funeral, which was a great honor. Her body was carried through the streets of Calcutta on a gun carriage, as thousands of people watched from the roadside. Leaders from all over the world attended the funeral mass, which was held in a sports stadium. Afterward, Mother Teresa was laid to rest beneath a simple stone slab in the Mother House.

"It's very sad that she died," said Hannah. "But what an amazing life she led. I mean, she started off as a simple nun and went on to become world famous!"

"Exactly," said Mr. Rummage. "And even though everyone missed her terribly, the work of the Missionaries of Charity went on after her death. And it still goes on today. There are now 600 houses in 130 countries, and about 4,000 Sisters, 400 Brothers, and thousands of other helpers. They still help poor people and lepers, but they also help the homeless, drug addicts, victims of war, and people with AIDS.

"That's it," said Digby, firmly. "I've decided."

"What now?" said Hannah, suspiciously.

"I'm not going to buy anything this week," said Digby, dropping his money into the alms bowl. "I'm giving my money to charity instead."

"Goody-goody," muttered Hannah.

"Very generous," said Mr. Rummage, rattling the bowl which was filling up nicely. "And now, you two, Saffron and I must get back to work. So goodbye until next week. I'll see you next Saturday for another story."

"Bye, Mr. Rummage! Bye, Saffron!" called Digby.

"Bye!" said Hannah, quickly dropping some coins into the alms bowl before anyone noticed.

# The making of a saint

## What is a saint?

For Christians, a saint is someone who has led an especially holy life and perhaps suffered for his or her religion. Some Christians pray to the saints and ask them for help and guidance. They also celebrate Saints' Days. Some saints are linked with particular jobs, events, or places. For example, St Benedict is the patron saint of school children.

The coat of arms of the Vatican City, Rome, in Italy—home of the Roman Catholic Church and the pope.

## Canonization

In the Roman Catholic Church, some holy people are declared to be saints, or canonized, after their death. There are several steps to becoming a saint.

The process usually begins five years after the person's death. Local bishops investigate the person's life and send their findings to the Vatican in Rome.

A group of cardinals, or senior priests, and other scholars approve the findings.

Then the pope declares the person to be "Venerable," which means that he or she is a role model of Roman Catholic qualities and virtues.

The next step is to find out if the person performed a miracle after his or her death. If they did, they are beatified and then given the title of "Blessed."

To become a saint, there must be proof of a second miracle done after the person's death.

Schoolchildren remember Mother Teresa in their prayers.

# Blessed Teresa of Calcutta

While she was alive, many people called Mother Teresa a living saint because of the good works she did. After her death in 1997, the Roman Catholic Church began the process of canonization to make her a saint.

First they needed to find a miracle performed by Mother Teresa after her death. In 2002, they discovered that an Indian woman had been cured of an illness by wearing a locket containing Mother Teresa's picture.

On October 19, 2003, Mother Teresa was officially beatified by Pope John Paul II and became the Blessed Teresa of Calcutta. In his speech, the pope said, "There is no doubt that the new Blessed was one of the greatest missionaries of the 20th century. The Lord made this simple woman, who came from one of Europe's poorest regions, a chosen instrument to proclaim the Gospel to the entire world—not by preaching but by daily acts of love towards the poorest of the poor."

A second miracle is needed before Mother Teresa can be made a saint.

# Mother Teresa's legacy

## A simple person

Agnes Bojaxhiu was born in one of the poorest and most politically unstable parts of Europe. A frail but deeply religious child, she left her home and family to follow her calling of becoming a nun and working among the world's poorest people. By the end of her life, she was seen by many people as a living saint, someone who saw "the image of God" in each person's face. From her humble beginnings, she went on to help and influence millions of people through her extraordinary and inspiring life.

From her early days in India, Mother Teresa dedicated her life to helping people who were shunned or neglected by society. These included the poorest of the poor, people who were homeless and dying, and people suffering from terrible diseases. Inspired by her firm belief in God, she tried to make their lives more bearable by showing them love and care when no one else would. Wherever she went, Mother Teresa never shied away from difficult or unpleasant situations. Today, the Missionaries of Charity continue her work around the world, bringing hope and comfort to millions of desperate people.

## Life is...

When she was in her seventies, Mother Teresa summed up her own attitude to life:

"Life is an opportunity, benefit from it.
Life is beauty, admire it.
Life is bliss, taste it.
Life is a dream, realize it.
Life is a challenge, meet it.
Life is costly, care for it.
Life is wealth, keep it.
Life is love, enjoy it.
Life is a promise, fulfill it.
Life is sorrow, overcome it.
Life is a song, sing it.
Life is a struggle, accept it.
Life is an adventure, dare it.
Life is luck, make it.
Life is too precious, do not destroy it.
Life is life, fight for it!"

# Glossary

**alms** Money or goods given as charity to the poor

**crucifix** An image or figure of Jesus on the cross

**leper** A person who suffers from leprosy

**leprosy** A long-lasting, mildly contagious disease caused by a bacteria that deform the skin, bones, and nerves so that victims lose their sense of feeling and/or become paralyzed; damaged or deformed body parts may fall off the body

**Muslim** A person who practices the Islam religion, which believes in Muhammad as the chief and last prophet of God

**nun** A woman who belongs to a religious order or congregation devoted to serving the poor or meditation, who lives according to vows of poverty, pure living, and devotion to God

**pilgrimage** A journey to a sacred place or shrine

**saint** A person whose faith and actions during his or her life caused them to be recognized by the church as holy people who can help and guide people on Earth

**sari** A dress worn mainly by the women of India and Pakistan, which is made up of a length of lightweight cloth with one end wrapped about the waist to form a skirt and the other draped over the shoulder or covering the head

**slum** A part of a city where a lot of poor people live either on the streets or in shacks or other poor-quality housing

**squalid** Dirty and wretched because of poverty or lack of care

# Index

Other characters in the Stories of Great People series.

PIXIE the market's fortuneteller sells incense, lotions and potions, candles, mandalas, and crystals inside her exotic stall.

PRU is a dreamer and Hannah's best friend. She likes to visit the market with Digby and Hannah, especially when makeup and dressing up is involved.

Mr. POLLOCK's toy stall is filled with string puppets, rocking horses, model planes, wooden animals—and he makes them all himself!

JAKE is Digby's friend. He's got a lively imagination and is always up to mischief.

KENZO the barber has a wig or hairpiece for every occasion, and is always happy to put his scissors to use!

BUZZ is a street vendor with all the gossip. He sells treats from a tray that's strapped around his neck.

COLONEL KARBUNCLE sells military uniforms, medals, flags, swords, helmets, cannon balls—all from the trunk of his old jeep.

Mrs. BILGE pushes her dustcart around the market, picking up litter. Trouble is, she's always throwing away the objects on Mr. *Rummage's* stall.

Mr. CLUMPMUGGER has an amazing collection of ancient maps, dusty books, and old newspapers in his rare prints stall.

CHRISSY's vintage clothing stall has all the costumes Digby and Hannah need to act out the characters in Mr. *Rummage's* stories.

YOUSSEF has traveled to many places around the world. He carries a bag full of souvenirs from his exciting journeys.